5 Simple Steps to Get Out of Debt

Live Debt-Free & Experience Financial Freedom

By Violet James, MSM

Maximum Potential, LLC

Cover Design by Violet James

Table of Contents

iv

INTRODUCTION

If you are one of the millions of people who have accumulated hundreds or even thousands of dollars of debt and want to successfully get control of your finances and live debt-free, then this simple, step-by-step plan is for you. It is crucial to have a strategic plan with set goals on how to get out of debt if you want to be victorious in living debt-free. You are at a huge advantage because you now have all the tools you need to change your situation with this proven, debt reduction strategy plan. Those who have a plan and set goals have a significantly higher percentage rate of accomplishing their desired goals.

Being in debt and owing money is very stressful and feels like you are carrying around a heavy burden. It can affect your emotions, health and relationships in a negative way. Also, if you are living paycheck to paycheck it can be very scary if you lose your job or something unexpected happens that causes the income to stop coming in. You are at a huge disadvantage when you owe money. You are at the mercy of the lender. A proverb states, "... the borrower is a servant to the lender." (Proverbs 22:7). It is important to make eliminating debt and being debt-free a priority so you can experience true financial freedom.

In this book, you will have a step-by-step debt reduction plan to follow. It is recommended that you take one step at a time and do the assignment/action plan for that step before you move on. When you have completed the steps and action plans, you will have control of your spending, have created a budget and have the skills to master your money.

Let's get started to financial freedom!

STEP #1

Let's Get Organized

"Out of debt, out of danger." ~ Proverb

The first step to getting out of debt is to get organized. It is important to know exactly how much money you owe to creditors. Many people have no idea what they owe. They are clueless as to the exact amounts of credit card debt they have to repay, how much they are getting charged in interest and their remaining balances due. Having a list of this information is crucial and will be very valuable for when you implement the pay-off debt plan in Step #5.

Assignment/Action Plan #1-
Prepare a Credit Card Liability List

Make a list of ALL credit card debt. DO NOT include any loans *(mortgage loans, auto loans, student loans, etc.)* or other expenses in this list. We will add those expenses in the next step.

Go gather all your statements, get a cup of coffee and start your list by recording each credit card debt. This step can be very stressful and painful but do not get discouraged. You can and will have financial freedom if you implement a plan and stick with it.

For each creditor that you owe, include the following information:

Name of Creditor
Remaining Balance Amount Due
Interest Rate
Minimum Monthly Payment Due

You can organize the debt by either highest to lowest interest rate OR lowest to highest remaining balance *(see examples)*. You will pay off the debt by using one of these methods. Some people like to pay off the smallest balance regardless of the interest rate because it makes them feel good to start getting rid of these smaller bills one at a time. However, many financial advisors recommend that you start with paying off the credit card with the highest interest rate first to save on interest charges. Either way, pick a method that you feel comfortable with.

After you have completed the list, be sure to add up the total amount you owe for all the minimum monthly payments due *(in the examples the total monthly credit card payment = $644.00).*

Following are Examples of Credit Card Liability Lists —

Example **Credit Card Liability List** *(highest to lowest interest rate)*

Creditor	Balance Due	Interest Rate	Min. Payment
Dept Store Credit Card	$1,450.00	24.90%	$75.00
Dept Store Credit Card	$927.36	21.90%	$65.00
Credit Card 1	$8,700.00	19%	$150.00
Credit Card 2	$455.00	12%	$25.00
Gas Card	$2,487.00	8.55%	$55.00
Store Card	$6,000.00	5.50%	$274.00
		Total Monthy Credit Card Payment =	$644.00

Example **Credit Card Liability List** *(lowest to highest balance due)*

Creditor	Balance Due	Interest Rate	Min. Payment
Credit Card 2	$455.00	12%	$25.00
Dept Store Credit Card	$927.36	21.90%	$65.00
Dept Store Credit Card	$1,450.00	24.90%	$75.00
Gas Card	$2,487.00	8.55%	$55.00
Store Card	$6,000.00	5.50%	$274.00
Credit Card 1	$8,700.00	19%	$150.00
		Total Monthly Credit Card Payment =	$644.00

NOTE: At this point you have an option to consider consolidating your credit card debt into one loan that offers a lower interest rate if you still have good credit/fico score. Tip: DO NOT get a home equity loan *(secured debt)* to transfer credit card debt that is unsecured debt. The difference between secured debt and unsecured debt is-- **secured debt** is guaranteed by an asset *(examples are mortgage and car loans- if you do not pay, the* *lender can take your house or car)* whereas with **unsecured debt** *(examples are personal loans and credit cards)* there is no collateral for the lender to take.

STEP #2

How Much Money is Coming in and Going Out

"You have to face it to erase it!" ~ Suze Orman

Before you can identify where to cut costs and how to budget your money, you first need to know exactly how much money is coming in and how much money is going out. You may be surprised by how much little expenses like coffee lattes and salons add up over time.

So, the next step is to prepare a Monthly Income/ Expense Statement. It's important to record how much money is coming in and how much money you are spending per month. If you are not sure exactly where your money is going each month, track your spending for a month or two by writing down every purchase and the amount spent until you have an accurate assessment of your spending THEN continue this next step's action plan.

Assignment/Action Plan #2

Prepare a Monthly Income / Expense Statement and Summary

First, prepare a **Monthly Income Statement**. **List all income** coming in per month *(include paychecks, unemployment checks, alimony/child support, social security, pension/retirement/IRA, dividends/interest, rental income, and any other income)*. Add the total monthly income.

Following is an Example of a Monthly Income Statement—

Monthly Income Statement

Income:

Paycheck

Unemployment Check

Alimony/ Child Support

Social Security

Retirement/IRA/Pension

Dividends/Interest

Rental Income

Misc. Income

Total Monthly Income _____

Next, prepare a **Monthly Expense Statement. List all monthly expenses** *(include mortgage /rent payments, auto loans, student loans, personal loans/home equity, utilities, telephone/cell, cable/internet, tithe/donations, insurance, grocery/food, child care, personal, entertainment, total credit card payment- from step#1, **escrow savings deposit and any other monthly expense).* Add the total monthly expenses.

Monthly Expense Statement

Expenses:
Mortgage Payment/ Rent

Auto Loan

Student Loan

Personal Loan

Home Equity Loan

Credit Card Payment *(from step#1)*

Telephone/ Cell Phones

Internet/ Cable

Heating /Gas

Electricity

Car Gas/ Repairs

Tithe/ Donations

Medical/ Dental

House Insurance

Car Insurance

Medical/ Health/ Dental Insurance

Life Insurance

Grocery/ Food

Child Care/Sports/Lessons

Personal/Clothing/Gifts

Entertainment

**Escrow Savings Deposit

Other Expenses

Total Monthly Expenses _____

**Escrow Savings Deposit--
Annual or Large, Irregular Bills -Property Taxes,
Car/ House Insurance, Repairs
(Take yearly total of these bills & divide by 12
for monthly amount due to be set aside and
deposited in a savings account)

Escrow Savings Deposit Expense-- set aside money per month for major bills that are due annually or at irregular times of the year *(examples include property taxes, insurance, repairs, etc.*). It is much easier to make small monthly payments instead of one large one-time payment. Every month put money in a savings account *(escrow account)* that you cannot use for anything else. This is known as putting money in escrow. Take the annual estimated costs of these expenses and total the yearly amount due for these bills and divide by 12 months to get the monthly escrow amount needed *(see example)*. Each month you will have a total amount *(escrow savings deposit)* to put aside in a savings account so when the bill comes due you will have the money to pay for it.

Escrow Savings Deposit Example-

Property Tax	$2650.00
Unexpected Car Repairs	$ 500.00
Insurance	$ 650.00
Total	$ 3800.00

A total of $3800.00 of estimated yearly expenses *($3800.00 divided by 12 months=*

$317 per month) can be broken down into $317.00 per month to be put into an escrow savings account. In your Monthly Expense Statement you would now add $317.00 *(example)* under the Escrow Savings Deposit expense.

After you have listed your income and expenses then it's time to **add up the monthly summary total.** You will either have excess money remaining or you will have a deficit *(shortage)*.

Following is an Example of a Monthly Summary-

Monthly Income / Expense Summary

Total Income _____
Total Expenses_____
Cash Excess or Deficit _____

STEP #3

Prepare a Monthly Budget- Part One

Increase Income

"A budget is telling your money where to go instead of wondering where it went."
~ John Maxwell

You will either have a monthly excess *(extra)* or deficit *(shortage)* of money. If you have an excess, then you can skip Step #3 and Step #4 and go directly to Step #5. However, I still highly recommend that you prepare a monthly budget to increase income and cut expenses even if you do have an excess. Most likely, if you are in debt, you have a deficit.

In the next two steps, you will prepare a monthly budget that will match *(equal)* your income to your expenses *(making ends meet)*. You will do this by increasing income and/or cutting expenses. **Your goal is to live within your means which is to break-even or to have an excess of money after all expenses are paid.**

Example:
Total Monthly Income $4,500.00
Total Monthly Expenses $4,500.00
Cash Excess or Deficit = $0 Break-even

If you are in a situation where you are in a deficit *(your income is not enough to cover basic living expenses)* then you will want to seek additional sources of income as well as cut expenses *(Step #4)*.

In this step, you will focus on how to earn extra income.

NOTE: As you brainstorm ideas and take action on earning additional income, continue with Step #4- cutting your expenses. Use your current Monthly Income amount or approximate the increased monthly income amount until you get an accurate figure to update.

Assignment/Action Plan #3
Increase Income

Find ways to increase your income. Get creative.

Examples to earn extra income-

If you can, try to take on an additional part-time job.

Many people are earning additional income from starting their own small business and working at home *(examples- home daycare, cleaning services, dog walking, tailoring, handyman, tutoring, etc.)*.

If you are a couple/married then you may want to consider having two incomes, if currently only one person is working. However, you would need to evaluate the pros and cons of doing this *(additional costs of child care & other expenses versus the additional income, lost family time, etc)*.

Today many people are making money online. Whether it's through a website, affiliate marketing or blogging, there are many, endless opportunities to start an online business.

If you are a good sales person and like to sell, then find a company that offers commission sales for selling their products *(examples of*

companies that look for sales representatives include:
www.Avon.com,
www.MaryKay.com,
www.Amway.com,
www.JuicePlus.com
(Note: Listing here does not imply endorsement).

Find small and large ticket items that you have and no longer use that you can sell at a garage sale or sell on **www.craigslist.org, www.ebay.com** or in your local classified ads.

STEP #4

Prepare a Monthly Budget- Part Two

Cut Expenses

"We buy things we don't need with money we don't have to impress people we don't like."
~Dave Ramsey

After completing Step #3 you should have an accurate figure of your monthly income. Your goal is to spend no more than your income *(what's coming in).* In this step, you need to get real serious about taking control of your spending and identifying where to cut costs. Your monthly expenses cannot be more than what your monthly income is. **Your goal is to live within your means which is to break-even or to have an excess of money after all expenses are paid.**

But before you can do that, you need to STOP all credit card spending. DO NOT add anymore debt to your credit cards. It's recommended that you cut up all credit cards so you can't use them anymore. If this is too drastic for you, then hide them where they are not easily accessible. You can make an exception to keep one credit card for emergencies only.

Assignment/Action Plan #4
Cut Expenses

Get your completed Monthly Expense Statement from Step #2. Review the list of expense items and identify where to cut costs. There are items that you cannot eliminate or reduce that are set prices like a mortgage payment, car payment, taxes, utilities, etc. However, there will be expenses that you can take out and eliminate *(usually entertainment and personal expenses)* or expenses that you can try to get monthly payment/rates reduced *(see examples)*.

This step is not easy and can be very painful because no one likes to give up things they enjoy and are accustomed to. But the hard reality is that you don't have the money for these items and you need to get serious about getting out of debt.

Let's get started with cutting expenses and remember your GOAL is to break-even *(income coming in is the same amount as expenses)* or to have an excess after all expenses are paid.

Examples of ways to cut expenses:

To lower **Insurance payments** *(house, car, health, medical),* you can increase your deductibles.   Example: $250 deductible increased to $1000 deductible can lower your monthly payment significantly.   The higher the deductible you choose, the lower the monthly payment.   Nevertheless, you should pick an amount that you are comfortable with in case something happens and you need to pay that deductible.

To lower **Telephone/Cell Phone, Internet, Credit Card, Cable Bills,** you can call their customer service to ask and negotiate for reduced rates, new promotional rates or different, less costly packages.   **TIP:** Before you call your provider, write down how much you are currently paying per month and how long you have been a customer.   When you call ask the rep what kinds of discounts are available and what they can do to help you reduce your monthly bill *(go on their website* *before you call and see what new special deals they are currently offering new customers).* Sometimes when you call your provider, the rep isn't too eager to help you with a discount but if you let them know you are considering canceling your service then the rep will transfer you to a retention specialist *(cancellation department).* These trained sales people are there to keep you from canceling your service so they will work with you to get you what you want.

To lower **Grocery/Food Bills,** determine your food budget for the month and divide by 4 weeks. This amount is the maximum you can spend on groceries for any given week. To make your dollar go farther at the grocery store, start clipping coupons and plan ahead. Make a list of the grocery items you will need and when shopping only purchase the items on the list to drastically cut the cost of impulse purchases. Also, never go grocery shopping when you are hungry. There are many really good, helpful websites that give you tips on how to save hundreds of dollars on groceries and where you can print coupons--
www.coupons.com
www.thekrazycouponlady.com

www.couponcabin.com
www.hip2save.com

To lower **Utility Bills** *(electrical, gas, etc.),* you can install efficient, energy saving products to reduce costs. Replace your standard light bulbs with fluorescent light bulbs to save on electricity. Installing a programmable thermostat to adjust and lower the temperature when you are at work and at night can save money on heating bills. Most utility companies offer a Comprehensive Home Assessment that includes an inspection of your home and a list of energy savings recommendations.

For **Student Loans**, you can ask for a deferment *(a postponement of loan payments).* For more information about deferring your loan go to **www.studentaid.ed.gov**

To lower **Entertainment, Clothing, Salon, Gift Bills and Other Personal Living Expenses**, you will have to make some sacrifices. These bills are usually the ones that get us into debt in the first place. However, these bills can be reduced or completely eliminated. Going out to eat is usually one of the highest monthly expenses people have. You can still go out to eat but limit it to what you can afford. Also, use coupons when going out to eat from websites like:

www.Restaurant.com
www.Groupon.com
www.Entertainment.com

Review all your entertainment and living expenses and be honest with yourself and drastically cut those expenses that you cannot afford.

Review your Monthly Expense Statement several times until you feel you have exhausted every possibility to cut and eliminate expenses. You will need to make the necessary adjustments to your expenses to break-even and spend only what income is coming in. After this step, you should have an updated, reduced Monthly Expense Statement. In addition, you will have an updated budget *(income statement and expense statement)* that matches your income to your expenses.
After increasing income and eliminating or reducing expenses, you should not be short of cash because now you have a good budget to

follow that ensures your income will cover all your living expenses. You will need to be COMMITED to your budget to have financial freedom.

It is recommended that you use cash only to pay for all expenses and learn to live on a cash budget only until you totally get out of debt and stop/control your credit card spending. This way you cannot spend more than you have coming in and you will not have the opportunity for impulse buying.

TIP: You can get envelopes *(glass jars or any other container)* and put labels on them *(expense items- groceries, gas, etc.)* and put the fixed cash budgeted amount for the week in the envelope. You can only spend what is in the envelope for that item that week.

NOTE: If after you have completed the following steps and find that you still have a large monthly deficit that seems impossible to manage, then you should seek financial help/assistance from a professional credit counselor or bankruptcy attorney.

STEP #5

Credit Card Pay-Off Strategy

"Credit buying is like being drunk. The buzz happens immediately, and it gives you a lift. The hangover comes the day after."
~Dr. Joyce Brothers

At this point, you should have a set monthly cash budget that you are committed to follow and live by until you are completely debt free.

Next, you will focus on creating a credit card pay-off plan/schedule to get rid of your credit card debt as quickly as possible. Credit card companies are continuously accruing interest on your balances and this is costing you more and more money.

In the previous step, you should have already called your credit card companies to negotiate a reduced interest rate. Even a 1% or 2% lower interest rate means that more of your payment is going towards paying off the balance.

Assignment/Action Plan #5
Create a Credit Card Pay-Off Schedule

Get your completed Credit Card Liability List from Step #1. In your Monthly Expense Statement, you should have recorded a Total Monthly Credit Card Payment which is the total amount you owe for all the minimum monthly payments due *(in the example from Step #1 the total monthly credit card payment = $644.00).*

Now let's create a Credit Card Pay-Off Schedule

Following is an Example of a Credit Card Pay-Off Schedule-

	Credit Card2	Dept Store	Dept Store	Gas Card	Store Card	Credit Card1	Monthly Payment
January	$25	$65	$75	$55	$274	$150	$644
February	$25	$65	$75	$55	$274	$150	$644
March	$25	$65	$75	$55	$274	$150	$644
April		$90	$75	$55	$274	$150	$644
May		$90	$75	$55	$274	$150	$644
June		$90	$75	$55	$274	$150	$644
July			$165	$55	$274	$150	$644
August			$165	$55	$274	$150	$644
September			$165	$55	$274	$150	$644
October			$165	$55	$274	$150	$644
November				$220	$274	$150	$644
December				$220	$274	$150	$644
January					$494	$150	$644
February					$494	$150	$644
March					$494	$150	$644
April						$644	$644
May						$644	$644
June						$644	$644

You will have several columns going across the paper. In the first column, list all the months of the year *(January, February, etc.)*. This column can extend 2-5 years depending on how much debt you have.

Next, list all your credit card debts across the top of the page in the next remaining columns- starting with either the highest interest rate or lowest remaining balance *(whichever method you used to create the Credit Card Liability List in Step#1)*. Record the minimum monthly payment for each debt and write that amount under the month. The last column is the total monthly credit card payment *(it should always add up to your Monthly Credit Card Payment expense- example total = $644.00)*. As you pay off the credit card in the first column, you then apply and transfer that amount of money you were paying to the next credit card debt/column and then the next and the next. Continue this payment schedule until ALL debts are paid off.

Example: When Credit Card2 in column 1 is paid off, you then add the $25 you were paying monthly toward the Dept. Store debt *($25 + $65 min. payment =$90)*. Now your new minimum monthly payment for Dept. Store will be $90 until this card is paid off.

TIP: Determine if you can afford to pay any extra that is above the minimum payment starting with the first debt/column. Apply any extra income to this balance *(extra money from garage sales, side jobs, tax return refund, etc.)*. You don't want to pay just the minimum payment because not only is interest accruing but it can take years to pay off. After you pay off the first debt, you will then be able to continue to pay more than the minimum payment on the next debt or so forth. Your goal is to pay your debt as quickly as possible but within a realistic time frame.

After all credit card debts are paid, apply that total monthly credit card payment *(example= $644)* towards paying off any other debts *(car loans, student loans, mortgage, etc.)* and investing for your future *(3-6 month emergency savings fund, retirement fund/IRA, college fund, etc.).*

Your goal is to get completely out of debt, invest for your future and continue to live within your means.

TIPS:
*Keep bank accounts *(savings, checking)* reconciled and balanced

*Annually review your credit report and fico score- www.annualcreditreport.com, www.freecreditscore.com

*Writing out your bills and adjusting your cash budget twice (2x) a month or weekly can help you be better organized and help keep you on budget

*Ideal ratios for income distribution– 10% for savings/future, 10% for personal spending, 10% tithe/giving, 70% bills

CONCLUSION

Staying Out of Debt

"There is no dignity quite so impressive, and no one independence quite so important, as living within your means." ~ Calvin Coolidge

Congratulations, you are on your way to being completely debt-free! By creating and following a solid budget, you have made eliminating debt and staying out of debt a priority. As you continue to resist credit card temptation and change your spending behavior, you will have made living debt-free your new lifestyle *(living within your means)*. Many people get out of debt only to get right back into it even worse than before. The reason they get right back into debt is because they did not change their spending behavior and made the huge mistake of not living on a budget. You now have a good budget to follow that will ensure that your income is spent wisely and that you will not get into this situation again. Stay positive, determined and consistent. You can do it! However, if you do mess up and spend more than your budget DON'T QUIT and give up, stick with it, get back on track and keep going. Be patient, persistent and encouraged because you are about to experience true financial freedom!

Resources:

Nonprofit Debt Management Programs:

National Foundation for Credit Counseling-
http://nfcc.org

Association of Independent Consumer Credit
Counseling Agencies- http://aiccca.org

About the Author

Violet James, MSM is an entrepreneur, marketing and business manager, award-winning web designer, and artist. She has over 20 years experience in business consulting, marketing and management. She is the cofounder and executive director of NewDayCounseling.org, BeHappy4Life.com and Christian-Kindle-Books.com.

Connect with Violet James

It is my sincerest desire and hope *5 Simple Steps to Get Out of Debt* has helped you to discover financial freedom and live debt-free. I would love to hear your testimonials and how you have been helped. You can send your testimonials, feedback and comments to me at:

 maxpotential312@gmail.com

I encourage you to share your experience, and I would truly appreciate if you would **write a review** on Amazon.com

My author profile:
http://www.amazon.com/author/violetjames

Join our *Words of Inspiration* page and Friend us on Facebook:
http://www.facebook.com/WordsOfInspiration

Follow and connect with us on Twitter:
http://www.twitter.com/behappy4lifeNDC

Visit our *Be Your Best* blog (offers RSS):
http://www.newdaycounselingcenter.blogspot.com

LinkedIn:
http://www.linkedin.com/in/violetjames

Other books by Violet James:

5 Step Marketing Plan: A Winning Marketing Strategy for Small Businesses